D1317845

PEOPLE DID WHAT
IN
ANCIENT GREECE?

Shalini Vallepur

Crabtree Publishing Company

www.crabtreebooks.com

CRABTREE
PUBLISHING COMPANY
WWW.CRABTREEBOOKS.COM

Published in Canada
Crabtree Publishing
616 Welland Ave.
St. Catharines, Ontario
L2M 5V6

Published in the United States
Crabtree Publishing
PMB 59051
350 Fifth Avenue, 59th Floor
New York, New York 10118

Published in 2020 by Crabtree Publishing Company

Author: Shalini Vallepur

Editorial director: Kathy Middleton

Editors: Madeline Tyler, Petrice Custance

Design: Dan Scase

Proofreader: Wendy Scavuzzo

Production coordinator and prepress: Tammy McGarr

Print coordinator: Katherine Berti

All facts, statistics, web addresses and URLs in this book were verified as valid and accurate at time of writing.

No responsibility for any changes to external websites or references can be accepted by either the author or publisher.

Printed in the U.S.A./122019/CG20191101

All images are courtesy of Shutterstock.com, unless otherwise specified. With thanks to Getty Images, Thinkstock Photo and iStockphoto. Front Cover – miniwide, Beskova Ekaterina, Jeff Bird. 4&5 – invisibleStudio, Marsyas, Philipp Foltz. 6&7 – delcarmat, Mitch Barrie, Zde. 8&9 – Eroshka, Mirror-Images, GalleriX. 10&11 – Claudia Paulussen, sebos, Le Musée absolu, SofiaV, art3, delcarmat, SunshineVector, Voropaev Vasiliy. 12&13 – Arne von Brill Photo, French royal collections, Walters Art Museum, blackboard1965, Jakob Suckale. 14&15 – Africa Studio, Louvre, Babich Alexander, Justin Norris, eAlisa, Naci Yavuz. 16&17 – delcarmat, CNG, Taras Dubov. 18&19 – Olhastock, Bibi Saint-Pol, Gilmanshin. 20&21 – Map_Peloponnesian_War_431_BC-fr.svg, MicroOne, Judith Swaddling, Marie-Lan Nguyen. 22&23 – Maxim Maksutov, matrioshka, Sudowoodo, tan_tan. 24&25 – Viacheslav Lopatin, Jastrow, 3DMI, DFLC Prints. 26&27 – garanga, anyaivanova, Katsiaryna Pleshakova, Kamira, Nigar Alizada. 28&29 – PONGSAKORN NUALCHAVEE, aquatarkus, Dmitry Minein, Olena Go, Denis Zyatkov. BullsStock, AliakseiZAN. Speech bubble – yana shypova. Background – Jeff Bird. Scroll – Gaidamashchuk.
Fruit vectors – Beskova Ekaterina

Library and Archives Canada Cataloguing in Publication

Title: People did what in ancient Greece? / Shalini Vallepur.
Names: Vallepur, Shalini, author.
Description: Series statement: People did what??? |
  Previously published: King's Lynn, Norfolk :
  BookLife Publishing, 2019. | Includes index.
Identifiers: Canadiana (print) 20190193069 |
  Canadiana (ebook) 20190193077 |
  ISBN 9780778774204 (hardcover) |
  ISBN 9780778774242 (softcover) |
  ISBN 9781427125101 (HTML)
Subjects: LCSH: Greece—Social life and customs—
  Juvenile literature. | LCSH: Greece—Civilization—To 146 B.C.—
  Juvenile literature.
Classification: LCC DF78 .V35 2020 | DDC j938—dc23

Library of Congress Cataloging-in-Publication Data

Names: Vallepur, Shalini, author.
Title: People did what in ancient Greece? / Shalini Vallepur.
Description: New York : Crabtree Publishing Company, 2020. |
  Series: People did what??? | Includes index.
Identifiers: LCCN 2019043948 (print) | LCCN 2019043949 (ebook)
  ISBN 9780778774204 (hardcover) |
  ISBN 9780778774242 (paperback) |
  ISBN 9781427125101 (ebook)
Subjects: LCSH: Greece--Civilization--To 146 B.C.--Juvenile
  literature.
Classification: LCC DF77 .V25 2020 (print) | LCC DF77 (ebook) |
  DDC 938--dc23
LC record available at https://lccn.loc.gov/2019043948
LC ebook record available at https://lccn.loc.gov/2019043949

CONTENTS

Welcome to Ancient Greece!

Χαῖρε! That means "hello" in Greek. When we talk about ancient Greece, we mean the time between the years 800 B.C.E. and 146 B.C.E.

To say "Χαῖρε," say "kai-ee-ruh."

CITY-STATES

Ancient Greece was made up of many villages. There were also **city-states** called *poleis*, or *polis* for singular. While there were many different poleis, all ancient Greeks shared the same **culture**. They spoke the same language and worshiped the same gods and goddesses. However, even though the poleis were made up of very similar people, they still got into wars with each other.

Delphi

Thebes

Marathon

Corinth

Athens

Mycenae

Olympia

Sparta

CITIZENS AND SLAVES

Each polis had citizens. Citizens were allowed to vote and had to fight in the army in times of war. Citizens from one polis could move to another, but they couldn't be citizens of more than one polis. They were considered foreigners and were called *metoikoi*.

Enslaved people had no freedom. They were forced to work without being paid. There were many enslaved people in ancient Greece, and most became slaves as prisoners of war. Some enslaved people worked in the houses of rich citizens. Others worked on farms or in mines.

Orphaned babies were sometimes taken in by citizens and brought up to be slaves.

FACT
There were around 100,000 citizens, 10,000 metoikoi, and 150,000 enslaved people in Athens in 350 B.C.E.

Vote for me and there will be treats for all!

DEMOCRACY

Athens was an important polis. In 507 B.C.E., Cleisthenes, the leader of Athens, brought in something called *demokratia*. Demokratia means "rule by the people," and in modern times it is called **democracy**. It was the first time that citizens could vote for who their leaders would be.

On Top of the World

Ancient Greeks believed in many different gods and goddesses. Each god or goddess looked after a certain part of life. They protected ancient Greeks when they needed help and punished them if they did something wrong.

The 12 Olympians were the main gods and goddesses. They lived at the top of Mount Olympus and looked down at the people living below.

Zeus – King of the gods, throws lightning bolts when angry

Hera – Goddess of marriage and wife of Zeus

Aphrodite – Goddess of love and beauty, wife of Hephaestus

Apollo – God of music and poetry, twin brother of Artemis

Ares – God of war and a very angry boy

Artemis – Goddess of hunting and protector of the world, twin sister of Apollo

Athena – Goddess of wisdom, crafts, and war, do not mess with her

Demeter – Goddess of harvest and grain

Dionysus – God of wine, festivals, and fun times

Hephaestus – God of blacksmiths, husband of Aphrodite

Hermes – God of travel and a speedy messenger

Poseidon – God of the sea, carries a trident, or three-pronged spear

WORSHIP

Ancient Greeks worshiped the gods and goddesses every day to keep them happy. This meant that they had many festivals and built many temples for them. They said prayers at home whenever they could.

Temple of Hera

It was up to the priests in temples to talk to the gods and receive important messages from them.

THE ORACLE OF DELPHI

An oracle was somebody who claimed to be able to see into the future and gave people advice. People visited oracles to find out what the gods and goddesses wanted them to do. A priestess of Apollo in the city-state of Delphi became very famous. There was a crack in the ground that let out smelly **fumes**. The oracle would sit on a three-legged chair and breathe the fumes to hear messages from the gods. Sometimes she went into a **trance**.

Hmm, let me see... the gods think... you stink.

The Gods Did What?

You did not mess with the gods. Ever. Unless you wanted a horrible punishment. Let's see some of the craziest punishments that the gods dished out in Greek mythology.

THE PECKING OF PROMETHEUS

Prometheus did us all a favor. The myth of Prometheus tells us that he stole fire from Mount Olympus and brought it down to the people below. Life for people changed, but Prometheus was in deep trouble. Zeus was so angry that he had Prometheus chained to a rock. An eagle visited Prometheus every day and pecked out and ate his liver. His liver grew back overnight, but the eagle came back and did it again. This happened every day for many years, until the hero Heracles killed the eagle!

A TASTY TALE

The gods loved King Tantalus so much that they invited him to fancy dinners on Mount Olympus. King Tantalus wanted to show off to his friends back home, so he stole ambrosia and nectar from the gods. The gods found out and punished King Tantalus by trapping him in a lake beneath a fruit tree. Whenever he reached for a piece of fruit or a drink of water, they moved out of his reach. King Tantalus was sentenced to be hungry and thirsty forever!

So close, yet so far...

8

How dare you think you're better than me!

Arachne was the best weaver on Earth. She couldn't help showing off her fine tapestry and told everybody that she was better at weaving than Athena—the goddess of weaving! It wasn't long before Athena heard all about Arachne's bragging. Athena decided to punish Arachne by turning her into a spider. Arachne lived out her days weaving webs.

LET THE BAD TIMES ROLL

King Sisyphus was a terrible king. He was cruel and unfair to his people and sometimes even killed them! Zeus decided to take charge and punish King Sisyphus. The king was forced to push a giant boulder up a steep mountain. Whenever he got near the top, the boulder rolled all the way down to the bottom, and King Sisyphus had to start all over again. He did it again and again and again. He's probably still doing it now!

Argh, here we go again.

9

The Naked Olympics

The Olympic Games were held in the town of Olympia to honor the gods and goddesses on Mount Olympus. Men from all over ancient Greece traveled to Olympia to compete in different sporting events. The Olympics were held every four years from 776 B.C.E. until 393 C.E., before starting again much later in 1896. In ancient Greece, everybody had to be naked when they were competing!

OLYMPIC EVENTS

- Running
- Jumping
- Chariot racing
- Horse racing
- Discus throwing
- Wrestling
- Boxing

Boxing

Laurel wreath

Discus thrower

Winners received money and wore special laurel wreaths on their heads.

MILO DID WHAT?

Milo was super strong. Many stories say that he trained by carrying an ox around on his shoulders. He was so strong that he won the Olympic wrestling event six times! Milo got his strength from massive meals. He could eat 40 pounds (18 kg) of meat in one sitting!

SUPER SWEAT

Athletes were usually strong and healthy, and many people believed their sweat had special powers.

You're too oily!

Before exercising, athletes covered themselves with olive oil. After exercising, the oil, along with sweat and dirt, was scraped off the athlete's body. This delightful mixture, called gloios, was packed into bottles, then sold to people as medicine.

Funky Philosophers

Many great **philosophers** lived in ancient Greece. Philosophers spent their lives studying the world and asking questions about the gods, people, and the way things worked. Socrates, Plato, and Aristotle were some great philosophers. However, there are a few philosophers who did some wacky things...

DIOGENES DID WHAT?

Diogenes was a philosopher who was part of a group called the Cynics. The Cynics believed that everybody should live in a simple way. Diogenes wanted people to go back to living a simple life close to nature. Diogenes was often called a dog because he didn't wear shoes, lived outside in a barrel, and pooped and peed in the streets!

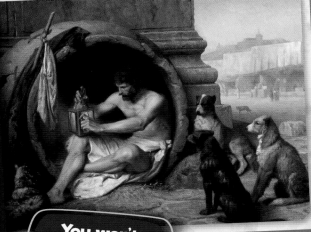

You won't make me laugh this time, donkey.

CHRYSIPPUS DID WHAT?

Chrysippus was a stoic philosopher. This meant that he believed people should be calm and not give in to their feelings. Stories say that Chrysippus died laughing, which was a bit odd for a stoic philosopher. He saw a donkey eat a fig and he then told a joke that was so funny that he couldn't stop laughing. He laughed so hard that he died!

Hippocrates was a good doctor. Before Hippocrates, everybody believed that people got sick because the gods were angry with them. Hippocrates thought that there must be another reason why people got terrible diseases and sicknesses.

Hippocrates is called the Father of Western Medicine.

THE FOUR HUMORS

Hippocrates believed the human body was made up of four humors, or liquids. They were black **bile**, yellow bile, blood, and **phlegm**. Each humor was connected to an emotion and a certain type of illness. Hippocrates believed that for a person to be healthy, all four humors had to be in balance.

Black bile – Believed to make people sad. Too much of this liquid caused digestive problems.

Blood – Believed to make people happy. Too much of this liquid caused a fever.

Yellow bile – Believed to make people angry. Too much of this liquid caused bowel problems.

Phlegm – Believed to make people calm. Too much of this liquid caused a cough or cold.

13

Doctor, Doctor

Thanks to Hippocrates, ancient Greek doctors had ways to balance the humors in times of illness...

RELEASE THE BLOOD

This headache will be the death of me.

If somebody had a bad headache, it was believed to be caused by too much blood. Bloodletting was the answer. This involved cutting the patient and letting some of the blood leave the body.

FANCY FARTS

Garlic was a wonderful treatment. Many doctors of the time believed that garlic could treat eye problems such as night blindness, or not being able to see well in the dark. Patients were told to apply garlic onto their eyelids!

But some doctors believed garlic ruined the balance in the body and led to all sorts of smelly gas problems...

Looks like we've got a trumpet in this band, folks.

A SNIFF...

Getting a diagnosis was easy in ancient Greece. A quick sniff and lick were all that was needed. Thanks to Hippocrates's teachings about the humors, doctors used their mouths and noses to taste and diagnose the illnesses of their patients!

Vomit is disgusting. But a simple lick of vomit could tell a doctor what was going on inside somebody. If the vomit was too sweet, then the patient definitely had some kind of illness.

Tasting pee was another good way to help get a diagnosis. Healthy pee tasted like fig juice!

I, Hippocrates, declare all doctors must lick vomit and drink pee.

Fresh fig juice, or fresh pee?

Today, people know it is a bad idea to drink pee!

Welcome to the Underworld

Ancient Greeks believed that people's souls went to the underworld when they died. The underworld was a place deep underground that was ruled by the god Hades. Hades was the brother of Zeus, and he decided where souls should go when they arrived in the underworld.

Most people went to the peaceful Asphodel Meadows.

People who were being punished by the gods were sent to the fields of punishment in Tartarus.

The bravest heroes went to the Elysian Fields.

ALL ABOARD

Cerberus, sit!

Hades's three-headed dog, Cerberus, guarded the gates to the underworld.

To get to the underworld, people had to cross the River Styx. Luckily, Hades had Charon the ferryman helping him out. People arrived at the River Styx and paid Charon a coin to be taken across the river in his little boat.

A PROPER BURIAL

Only those who were buried properly could make it to the underworld. There were many rituals that were carried out when somebody died. One of the most important rituals was giving the dead person a coin to pay Charon with. A coin was placed in or on the mouth of the dead person before they were buried.

Coins

If somebody was buried without a coin, they couldn't pay Charon to get to the underworld and would drift around hopelessly for 100 years.

STOP THE ZOMBIES!

But I'm not dead yet!

There were many beliefs about death in ancient Greece. Many people were scared of turning into zombies after they died. There was a simple answer to that. Putting large stones and pots on top of dead bodies stopped them from getting up. Perfect!

Gruesome Games and Terrific Toys

GET PIGGY WITH IT

Ancient Greeks loved to play *episkyros*. It's believed that the ball was made from a pig's bladder. The bladder was blown up and then shaped into a ball.

Oink

Soccer and football grew from games such as episkyros!

HOW TO PLAY EPISKYROS

Can I have a try?

- Get into two teams. Each team must have between 12 and 14 players.
- Draw a long line across the middle of the field.
- Each team stands on one side of the line in the middle.
- Each team draws a line behind where they are standing.
- Try to get the ball behind the other team's back line.
- Do whatever it takes to win!

HELLO TOYS

Ancient Greek children had plenty of toys to keep them entertained. All the cool kids had a yo-yo. Ancient Greek yo-yos were made of wood or **terracotta**. They were usually decorated with pictures of the gods and goddesses. A lot of children had dolls, too. Dolls were usually made of terracotta and some of them even had hair. Human hair was used to give dolls a fancy look.

Yo-yo Olympics here I come.

Horse on wheels

Terracotta doll

Buffalo on wheels

GOODBYE TOYS

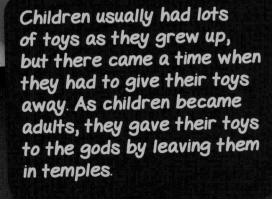

Children usually had lots of toys as they grew up, but there came a time when they had to give their toys away. As children became adults, they gave their toys to the gods by leaving them in temples.

The goddess Artemis was the protector of girls. When a girl was old enough to marry, she offered her dolls and toys to Artemis.

This Is Sparta

Sparta was a great city-state in ancient Greece. Its army was famous and feared by everybody for being strong, tough, and brutal. But what exactly did the Spartans do to their children to turn them into fighting machines?

MACEDONIA

Mount Olympus △

Troy

AEGEAN SEA

Delphi

Thebes
Salamis
Corinth
Athens
Olympia
Mycenae
Argos

ATTICA

Ephesus

Miletus

Pylos
Sparta
Cape Sounion
Delos

IONIAN SEA

Sparta

ARE YOU TOUGH ENOUGH?

Newborn babies were tested to see if they were strong enough to handle life in Sparta. Spartan soldiers checked the baby to see if it was strong and healthy. Some babies were even bathed in wine instead of water as a test!

Some parents left their newborn baby outside for a night. The baby was a real Spartan if it was alive the next morning.

Spartan citizens had to be strong and ready to defend Sparta in times of war. This meant that Spartan girls were expected to be just as strong as the boys. Spartan girls started school when they were seven years old.

The Spartans knew that strong and healthy girls grew up to have strong babies.

Spartan girls were trained in sports such as wrestling and gymnastics. They often exercised naked outside. They also learned about music, art, and history. This was different from the rest of ancient Greece, where girls weren't really allowed to do much at all.

AT THE AGOGE

Like Spartan girls, Spartan boys started school when they were seven. They went to the agoge. The *agoge* was a special school that trained boys to be soldiers. The boys lived in large **barracks**. They became soldiers at 20 and stayed in the army until they were 60.

FACT
Spartan soldiers were called hoplites.

Training was terrible and tough. The boys were given scraps of food to eat. They had to sneak around and find their own food or steal it. If they got caught stealing food, they were beaten by their trainers.

Red cloak

Spartan shield

When the boys turned 12, they stopped wearing clothes. They were only allowed to wear a red cloak and were forced to sleep outside on the ground on a bed made from **reeds**. Talk about tough!

TERRIBLE TALES

Many tales were told to inspire Spartans to be brave even when they were in pain. One tale told the story of a Spartan boy and a fox...

One day, a Spartan boy was hungry. He snuck around looking for food and came across a fox. The boy snatched the fox in a hurry.

Suddenly, a trainer walked by. The boy didn't want to get caught looking for food, so he hid the fox under his shirt. The boy stood perfectly still as the trainer looked him up and down. The fox scratched and scratched the boy's belly, but the boy wouldn't tell the trainer that he had been looking for food. He stayed still and pretended that he wasn't hurt.

But the boy was hurt. Eventually, the boy died from the fox's scratches. A true Spartan hero!

Theater Trips

CITY DIONYSIA

In Athens, a festival called City Dionysia was held every March to honor the god Dionysus. As part of the celebration, plays were performed. People gathered at the Odeon theater to watch **tragedies** and comedies.

FACT
Around 5,000 people could fit in the Odeon in Athens.

TOTALLY TRAGIC

A tragedy was a serious play. It told stories from mythology and usually something bad happened to the main character. A favorite play of the ancient Greeks was called Oedipus the King. In the play, poor Oedipus had to solve a nasty riddle. Oh, he also killed his father. Talk about tragic!

I told you already, your riddles are terrible.

A LAUGHING MATTER

Everybody loved a good comedy. Comedies were funny plays. Actors wore fancy clothes and all sorts of wacky things happened. Usually, there were only three actors in a play. A big of group of people, called the chorus, all sang songs, danced, or spoke together during the play.

Comedies were usually about silly things, and characters dressed very silly, too.

ANCIENT ACTORS

Only men were allowed to be actors. It didn't matter if the play had female characters in it. They wore big masks, and some wore special shoes called *cothurni* that had material added to the bottom to make the actor taller. That way, everybody watching the play could see the actors.

Cothurni

Comic mask

Tragic mask

Arty Farty Greeks

Ancient Greeks loved art. Whether it was theater, statues, paintings, or pots, they loved it all. Art could be seen all around ancient Greece.

PHIDIAS DID WHAT?

Phidias was a great sculptor. He made a grand statue of Athena in Athens and was chosen to make a statue of Zeus for the Temple of Zeus in Olympia. The statue of Zeus was huge. It was 40 feet (12 m) tall and had Zeus sitting on a grand throne made of gold and ivory.

The Parthenon in Athens shows off ancient Greek architecture.

The statue of Zeus was so impressive that people traveled from far and wide to see it.

CRAZY FOR POTS

Ancient Greeks used pots for everything. There was a lot of clay in Greece, so potters could make lots and lots of pots. Most pots were decorated simply, but many had pictures painted on them. There were different types of pots for storing drinks and water.

Paintings on pots told stories about the gods, and many showed everyday life.

POTS AND POOP

Rich people had all sorts of tools to wipe themselves after a you-know-what. Sponges were popular, but not everybody could afford them. Luckily, pots were cheap, and everybody had them. Smash up a pot and you're left with shards. A big shard of pottery was perfect for scraping away at the butt.

Hair Care and Messy Makeup

PRETTY IN POOP

Sometimes, the best beauty treatments are the smelliest. Crocodile poop was a popular skin cream. It was believed to stop people from getting wrinkles.

This smells amazing.

For best results, mix a huge amount of crocodile poop with mud, and stick it in the bathtub for a whole-body experience.

IT'S ALL IN THE UNIBROW

It suits me, doesn't it?

Ancient Greek women loved having one big eyebrow. Unibrows were a sign of cleverness. A bit of soot could turn two pale eyebrows into one big fat brow! Fabulous!

LIGHT HAIR

It's fun to change your hair color. A lot of people wanted to make their hair lighter, or blonder. There was a very simple way to do this.

Ancient Greeks poured vinegar on their hair. Then, they sat outside in the sunshine. It stunk and it stung when it got on the skin, but it lightened their hair color slightly.

Vinegar + Sunshine =

BUSHY BEARDS

Greek gods and heroes had nice, curly beards that Greek men were jealous of. The bigger the beard, the manlier the man was. Men took a pair of tongs, heated them up, and used them to curl their beards to look just like Zeus.

Tongs

LEARNING MORE

BOOKS

Hudak, Heather C. *Forensic Investigations of the Ancient Greeks.* Crabtree Publishing, 2019.

Malam, John. *Ancient Greece Inside Out.* Crabtree Publishing, 2017.

Samuels, Charlie. *Ancient Greece.* Franklin Watts, 2015.

WEBSITES

Visit this site to learn more about the first Olympic games.
www.kids.nationalgeographic.com/explore/history/first-olympics/

Learn more about ancient Greece here.
www.coolkidfacts.com/ancient-greece/

This site has some cool facts about life in ancient Greece.
www.historyforkids.net/ancient-greece.html

GLOSSARY

ambrosia The special food that only the gods and goddesses ate

architecture The design and style of a building or buildings

barracks Large buildings where soldiers live

bile A yellow or greenish fluid in the stomach which helps to break down food

blacksmiths People who make things out of iron

bladder The organ that holds and releases urine

chariot A horse-drawn cart with two wheels, used in ancient racing

city-states Cities that have their own laws and leaders which are separate from the rest of the country

culture The ways of life and traditions of a group of people

democracy A system in which people vote for their leaders and have a say in how the government is run

diagnosis When a doctor discovers what disease or illness a patient has

discus A heavy disk thrown by an athlete

fumes Smoky gases

harvest To gather a crop

honor To show respect to something or someone

ivory A hard, white substance that forms on elephant tusks

mythology Very old stories about gods, goddesses, and heroes

nectar The special drink that only the gods and goddesses drank

philosophers People who teach or practice philosophy, or the study of thought

phlegm Mucus from the nose or throat

reeds Tall grasses that grow in swamps

rituals Specific actions that take place during religious ceremonies

soot A black powder that is formed when things are burned

tapestry Cloth that has a picture or pattern woven onto it

temples Places of worship

terracotta A type of clay that is a deep brownish-red

tragedies Types of plays that have a sad ending, usually showing the downfall of a main character

trance A state that seems to be between being asleep and awake, in which people might act differently than usual

weaver A person who weaves thread to make fabric

INDEX